ME COUNTING TIME
TIME
From Seconds to Centuries

ME COUNTING TIME

From Seconds to Centuries

by Joan Sweeney   illustrated by Annette Cable

SCHOLASTIC INC.

New York   Toronto   London   Auckland   Sydney
Mexico City   New Delhi   Hong Kong

For my brothers, Ed and Jim,
who gave me the answers I needed just in time!
—J.S.

For Grandma Myers,
love, A.C.

ISBN 0-439-22129-3

Text copyright © 2000 by Joan Sweeney.
Illustrations copyright © 2000 by Annette Cable.
All rights reserved.
Published by Scholastic Inc., 555 Broadway, New York, NY 10012,
by arrangement with Crown Publishers, Inc.,
a Random House Company.
SCHOLASTIC and associated logos are trademarks and/or
registered trademarks of Scholastic Inc.

12 11 10 9 8 7 6 5 4 3   1 2 3 4 5 6/0

Printed in the U.S.A.   14

First Scholastic printing, September 2001

This is me. I'm inviting my friends to my birthday party.
I'm going to be seven years old.

Just think—seven candles for seven years.
But a year isn't a candle, a year is a measurement of time.

Time comes in different amounts—seconds, minutes, hours, days, and more. Here's how I tell them apart.

First I think of the blink of an eye. That's about one second of time. I can count seconds by saying "one Mississippi, two Mississippi."

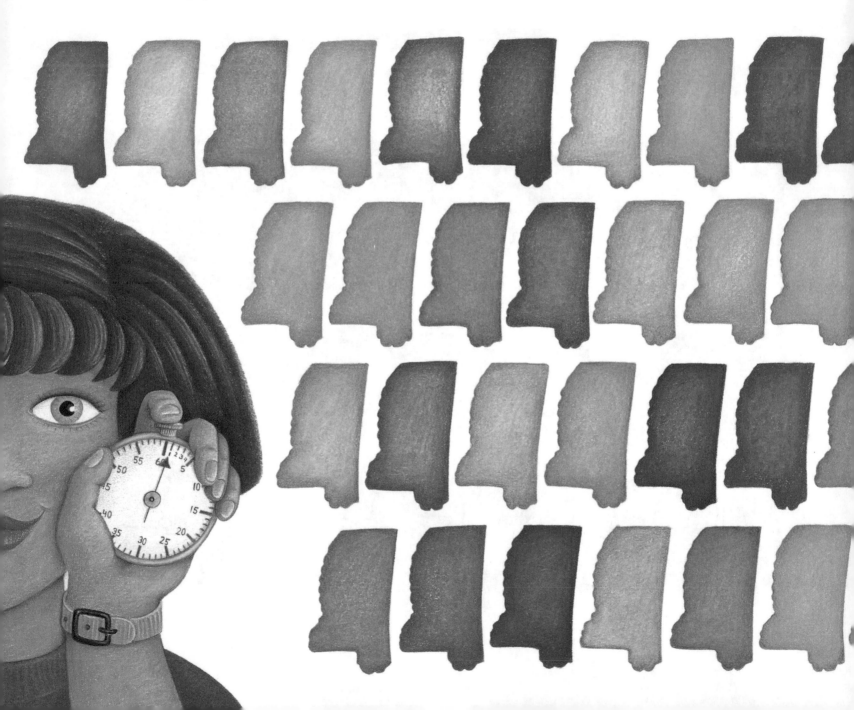

Then I think of *sixty seconds*. That's one minute of time.
I can write an invitation to my party in one minute!

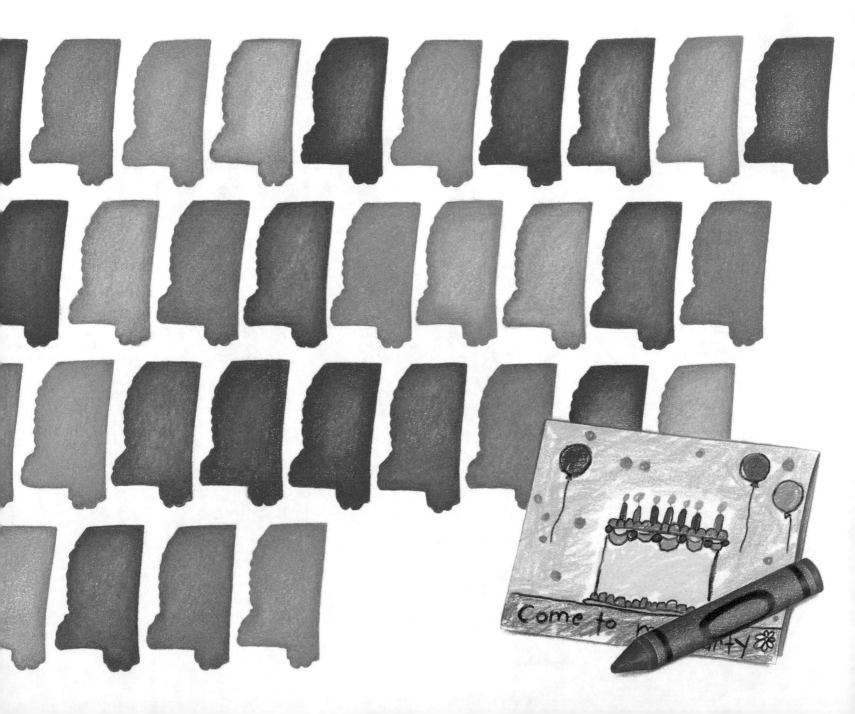

Then I think of *sixty minutes*. That's one hour of time—
the time it takes to make a birthday cake!

Then I think of *twenty-four hours.* That's one day.
The earth rotates once every day.

Then I think of *seven days*.
That's one week.

Sunday

Monday

Tuesday

Wednesday

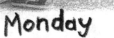
Thursday

Friday

Saturday

Then I think of *four weeks*. That's about one month. Most months are just over four weeks. Only February is four weeks *exactly*—except during leap year. Then it's four weeks plus one day!

Then I think of *twelve months*. That's one year.
From winter to spring to summer to fall.

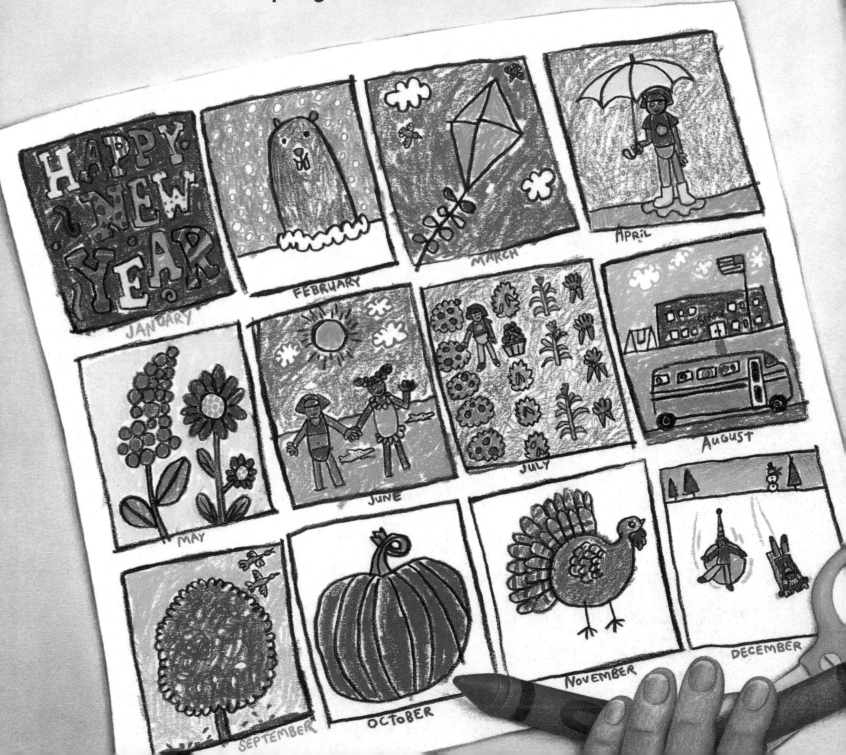

1 year

2 years

3 years

4 years

5 years

6 years

7 years

8 years

9 years

10 years

Then I think of *ten years*. Ten years is called a decade—even longer than I've been alive.

And then I think of *ten decades*. One hundred years. That's one century. Long enough for a tree to grow real tall.

A castle built in the year 1000.

Sand Castle, Virginia Beach 2000

Then I think of *ten centuries*. That's the same as one millennium. One thousand years!

Imagine. 31,556,926,000 blinks of an eye!
That's a long, long time.

A lot longer than seven years! So how do I get from
a millennium to my time? From a millennium to *now*?
Here's how.

A **millennium** ago, someone built a Viking ship like this. Now it would be one thousand years—ten centuries—old! A **century** ago, my great-great-grandpa had this picture taken. Now it's one hundred years old.

A **decade** ago, my nana sewed
this wedding dress for my mother.
Now it's ten years old.

A **year** ago, my family moved to our brand-new house.
Now it's twelve months old.

About a **month** ago, my cat had kittens.
Now they're four weeks old.

A **week** ago, I got new soccer shoes. Now they're seven days old.

A **day** ago, I painted this picture.
Now it's twenty-four hours old.

My dad can make my birthday cake in one **hour**. An hour is sixty minutes. A **minute** is sixty seconds. And a **second** is like the blink of an eye.

In seven days, I'll be seven years old.
Seven candles. 220,898,482 blinks of an eye!

I can't wait for my party.
I'm going to have the time of my life!

TIME

60 seconds = 1 minute

60 minutes = 1 hour

24 hours = 1 day

7 days = 1 week

4 weeks = about 1 month

12 months = 1 year

10 years = 1 decade

100 years = 1 century

10 centuries = 1 millennium